WORLD WAR TWO
HISTORY IN AN HOUR

Also in the *History in an Hour* series

World War Two

History in an Hour

RUPERT COLLEY

WILLIAM
COLLINS

William Collins
An imprint of HarperCollins*Publishers* Ltd
77–85 Fulham Palace Road
Hammersmith, London W6 8JB
www.harpercollins.co.uk

Visit the History in an Hour website:
www.historyinanhour.com

Published by William Collins in 2013

First published as an eBook by Harper*Press* in 2011

1

A catalogue record for this book
is available from the British Library

ISBN 978-0-00-753912-3

Set in Minion by FMG using Atomik ePublisher from Easypress

MIX
Paper from
responsible sources
FSC™   FSC® C007454
www.fsc.org

Contents

Introduction

Lasting six years and a day (until the formal surrender of Japan), the Second World War saw the civilian, both young and old, fighting on the front line. Civilian deaths accounted for 5 per cent of those killed during the First World War; but during the Second, of the 50 million-plus killed, they made up over 66 per cent. During the 2,194 days of the conflict, a thousand people died for each and every hour it lasted. With eighty-one of the world's nations involved, compared to twenty-eight during the First World War, this was a world war in the truest sense.

Germany Invades Poland:
'This is how I deal with any European city'

The Nazi–Soviet Non-Aggression Pact, signed on 23 August 1939, allowed Hitler to pursue his ambitions in the east without fear of Russian interference; ambitions that included the destruction of Poland and the subjugation of its people. The attack on Poland began at 4.45 on the morning of Friday, 1 September 1939.

The Germans, not intending to be bogged down again in a war of trenches and stalemate, swept aside all resistance in a lightning war of blitzkrieg, using technological military advances, co-ordinated attacks and abrasive speed. Following up the rapid advances, German forces engaged in brutality, executions and merciless aggression against the civilian population.

Neville Chamberlain, who had been Britain's Conservative prime minister since 1937, and who five months earlier had guaranteed the Poles assistance if attacked, dutifully declared war on Germany on 3 September, followed, six hours later, by the French.

The British contribution to the Polish cause was not with arms, nor soldiers, nor aid, but with leaflets – by the million, dropped by plane over Germany, urging the population to stand up against Hitler and the war.

On 17 September, as the German war machine advanced its way towards Warsaw, the Soviet Union, as secretly agreed in the Non-Aggression Pact, attacked from the east. Crushed between two totalitarian heavyweights, Poland crumbled, and on the twenty-seventh, Warsaw surrendered. Agreeing on the partition of Poland, the Germans and Russians then set about the total subjugation of the defeated population. Villages were razed, inhabitants massacred, the Polish identity eradicated; and in towns, such as Lodz, Jews were herded into ghettos before eventual transportation to the death camps. With his first objective achieved, Hitler visited Warsaw on 5 October, and casting a satisfied eye over the devastated capital, declared: 'this is how I deal with any European city'.

The Finnish–Soviet War: The 'Winter War'

Stalin, knowing that his country's pact with Germany would not last indefinitely, sought a buffer zone against any future German attack. By June 1940, he had bullied Estonia, Latvia and Lithuania into co-operation, swiftly followed by full annexation. Finland, however, resisted, preferring to fight than submit to Soviet demands. The 105-day 'Winter War' started with Russia's attack on Finland on 30 November 1939. Russia, expecting an easy victory as the Germans had had over the Poles, was soon disabused of this idea, underestimating Finnish bravery, tenacity and expertise at guerrilla warfare.

This, together with the Soviet Union's lack of military proficiency, following Stalin's military purge of the 1930s, and poor equipment that froze in the plummeting temperatures, meant the Soviets learnt a hard but useful lesson, eventually subduing the Finns in March 1940 by sheer weight of numbers.

The Norwegian Campaign: 'Missed the bus'

The supply of iron ore from Sweden to Germany via the northern Norwegian port of Narvik was essential to the German war machine. Both the Germans and British decided to take Narvik, the former to protect its supply route, the latter to disrupt it. When, on 8 April 1940, British ships started laying mines off the Norwegian coast, Chamberlain crowed that Hitler had 'missed the bus'.

But the Germans advanced swiftly into Scandinavia, forcing Denmark into a rapid surrender and compelling neutral Norway to take up arms as, one by one, her ports fell to the Germans. The British response, although fast, was dogged by inefficiency and disruption, with troops landing in snowy Norway without skis and provided only with tourist maps. When, on 10 May, Germany attacked Holland and Belgium, British forces in Norway were evacuated to the Low Countries, leaving Norway to fall under

German control and to be ruled by the Norwegian Nazi, Vidkun Quisling.

Winston Churchill, as First Lord of the Admiralty, took responsibility for the Norwegian debacle, but it was Chamberlain, as prime minister, who fell. Unable to form a coalition government, he was forced to resign amidst shouts in the House of Commons of 'Go, go, go!'. He was replaced, ironically, by Churchill. The date, 10 May, was the day that Hitler unleashed blitzkrieg south of the Channel. Six months later, Chamberlain was dead.

The Fall of France: 'France has lost a battle but France has not lost the war'

The period from the beginning of the war to 10 May 1940 was known in Britain as the 'phoney war', when the conflict still seemed far away. Children were evacuated to the countryside, rationing was introduced, as were evening blackouts and the carrying of gas masks.

Belgium, overwhelmed by the German advance, appealed to the Allies for assistance. The British and French responded by moving into Belgium to counter the German attack. Along the Franco-German border the French fielded a weaker force, putting faith in the Maginot Line, a defensive 280-mile-long fortification, built in the early 1930s as protection against the Germans. The Germans rendered it obsolete within a morning in May 1940 by merely skirting around the north of it, through the Ardennes forest, which, because of its rugged terrain, the French considered impassable. Reaching the town of Sedan on the French side of the

Ardennes on 14 May and brushing aside French resistance, the Germans pushed, not towards Paris as expected, but north, towards the English Channel, forcing the Allies further and further back. In 1916, the Germans had failed to take Verdun despite ten months of trench warfare; in May 1940, it took them one day.

In Holland, Rotterdam was heavily bombed and, on 15 May, the Dutch, fearing further losses, capitulated. On 28 May Belgium also surrendered. Allied forces, with their backs to the sea in the French coastal town of Dunkirk, were trapped. But the Germans, poised to annihilate the whole British Expeditionary Force, were inexplicably ordered by Hitler to halt outside the town. Between 26 May and 3 June, over 1,000 military and civilian vessels rescued and brought back to Britain 338,226 Allied soldiers. This was not achieved without scenes of panic, broken discipline and soldiers shot by their officers for losing self-control. Meanwhile, Hitler's generals watched, puzzled and ruing an opportunity missed.

On 4 June in the House of Commons, Churchill was careful not to call the 'miracle of Dunkirk' a victory but merely a 'deliverance'. He continued to give his famous 'We shall fight on the beaches' speech, concluding with the immortal words, 'We shall never surrender'. However, the French saw it somewhat differently – with the Germans closing in on Paris, they considered the Dunkirk evacuation a huge betrayal.

On 10 June, Italy declared war on the Allies. Four days later, Hitler's forces entered a largely deserted Paris, over 2 million Parisians having fled south. Soon the swastika was flying from the Arc de Triomphe.

On 16 June, the French general, Charles de Gaulle, escaped France to begin his life of exile in London. He was later sentenced to death – *in absentia* by the Vichy government. From London, de Gaulle broadcast a declaration, asserting that: 'France has lost a battle but France has not lost the war … The flame of French resistance must not and shall not die.' His words became the battle cry of the Free French movement.

Also on 16 June, the French prime minister Paul Reynaud resigned, to be replaced by 84-year-old Marshal Philippe Pétain, hero of the 1916 Battle of Verdun. Pétain's first acts were to seek an armistice with the Germans and order Reynaud's arrest. On 22 June, fifty miles north-east of Paris, the French officially surrendered, the ceremony taking place in the same spot and in the same railway carriage where the Germans had surrendered in 1918. Straight afterwards, on Hitler's orders, the railway carriage and the monuments commemorating the 1918 signing were destroyed. The following day Hitler visited Paris, his only trip to the capital, for a whistle-stop sightseeing tour of the city. On viewing Napoleon's tomb, he said: 'That was the greatest and finest moment of my life.' Before departing, he ordered the demolition of two First World War monuments, including the memorial of Edith Cavell, the British nurse shot by the Germans in Brussels in October 1915.

Pétain and his puppet government ruled from the spa town of Vichy in central France. The Vichy government actively did the Nazis' dirty work: conducting a vicious civil war against the French Resistance, implementing numerous anti-Jewish laws, and sending tens of thousands of Jews to the death camps.

In July 1940, Churchill established the Special Operations Executive (SOE) to help resistance groups in France and elsewhere in Europe in the work of sabotage and subversion. In October 1940, Pétain met Hitler, and although Pétain opposed Hitler's demands that France should participate in the attack on Britain, photographs of the two men shaking hands were soon seen across the world – evidence of Vichy's complicity with the Nazis.

In July 1940, Churchill issued an ultimatum to the admiral of the French fleet docked in Mers-el-Kebir, Algeria – to hand the ships over to the British or scuttle them to prevent them from being used by the Kriegsmarine, the German navy. When the admiral refused to comply, Churchill ordered the Royal Navy to open fire, killing 1,297 French sailors. The incident served to sever relations between Vichy and Britain.

The Channel Islands were occupied by a German garrison from 30 June 1940 until the German surrender in May 1945. The only part of Great Britain to be occupied by the Germans throughout the war, there was almost one German for every two islanders. The islands were not of any strategic importance, but occupation of British territory was considered symbolically important to the Germans. Food supplies, delivered from France, were severely curtailed after the Normandy invasion of June 1944, and although the occasional Red Cross ship got through, by the time of liberation both the Germans and the islanders were on the point of starvation.

The Battle of Britain and the Blitz: 'It can only end in annihilation for one of us'

With Poland, Norway, Denmark, Belgium, Holland and France under Nazi control, Britain now faced the German onslaught alone. Operation Sea Lion, Germany's codename for the invasion of Britain, was quietly announced on 16 July. Hitler decreed that, as a prelude to a full-blown invasion, the German air force, the Luftwaffe, would destroy the RAF's air superiority over Britain. The following day, Hitler issued Britain a peace offering, his 'last appeal to reason': 'It can only end in annihilation for one of us. Mr Churchill thinks it will be Germany. I know it will be Britain.' Many in Parliament were tempted; Churchill was not.

The main thrust of Hitler's air assault, the commencement of the Battle of Britain, began on 13 August, the 'Day of the Eagle', when 1,485 German aircraft attacked Britain's coastal airfields. During the next month, the RAF and the Luftwaffe fought above the fields of south-east England in a series of dogfights where the average life expectancy of a British pilot was four to five weeks.

But the RAF enjoyed certain advantages of flying over home ground: if a British pilot had to bail out, he at least parachuted on to British soil and could return to the fight, unlike his German counterpart who, on landing, was whisked off into captivity. And, unlike the Luftwaffe, the RAF pilot was not subject to anti-aircraft fire; the British, by this stage, were using radar (still a comparatively new invention), and had learnt, through the team at Bletchley Park in Buckinghamshire, to decrypt Germany's Enigma codes. Bletchley Park knew, for example, of Operation Sea Lion before many of Hitler's generals did.

On 23 August, as it was returning from a sortie over Britain, a Luftwaffe patrol got lost and mistakenly bombed Croydon on the outskirts of London. The RAF bombed Berlin on 25 August. The damage was insignificant but Hitler, enraged, ordered the bombing of London. Between 7 September 1940 and 16 May 1941, the people of London and many other British cities as far north as Glasgow endured the Blitz, a sustained campaign of bombing.

After May 1941, the Luftwaffe was diverted to the Soviet Union. In just one night, 14 November 1940, 440 German bombers dropping over 1,000 tons of explosives destroyed Coventry, killing 568 people and seriously injuring 863. Altogether, during the Blitz, over 40,000 were killed and almost 50,000 injured. But if the aim was to destroy resolve, it failed: the bombings merely strengthened it. For Londoners, the sight of Churchill, and on another occasion, the King and Queen stepping through the devastation and talking to the locals certainly helped boost morale. After Buckingham Palace had been hit, Queen Elizabeth said: 'I'm glad we've been bombed – now I feel we can look the East End in the face.'

A second unintended consequence of Hitler's decision to target civilians was to give the RAF time to regroup and prepare for the next onslaught. That attack came on 15 September, now known as Battle of Britain Day, when the Luftwaffe, believing that the

RAF was on its knees, launched a concentrated attack on southeast England. The RAF doggedly fought them off and the Battle of Britain was effectively over. Two days later, Hitler postponed Operation Sea Lion indefinitely. As Churchill stirringly said, 'Never in the field of human conflict was so much owed by so many to so few.'

The Mediterranean: 'One moment on a battlefield is worth a thousand years of peace'

Since coming to power in 1922, Benito Mussolini fancied himself as a modern-day Caesar and Italy his Roman Empire. In his bid to start building an empire worthy of his ancient predecessors, Italy grabbed for itself Ethiopia (then Abyssinia) in 1936 and Albania in 1939. On 16 May 1940, Churchill had pleaded with Mussolini not to declare war: 'Is it too late to stop a river of blood from flowing between the British and Italian peoples?' he asked. But just three weeks later, on 10 June, with France only days from capitulating, Mussolini declared war on the Allies, boasting, 'One moment on a battlefield is worth a thousand years of peace', and prompting Hitler to comment: 'First they were too cowardly to take part. Now they are in a hurry so that they can share in the spoils.' On 28 October, from their bases in Albania, Italy attacked Greece. Mussolini's dreams of empire soon unravelled in humiliating fashion. With insufficient weapons, lack of winter clothing and supplies, the Italians faltered within fifty miles. The Greeks, with help from the British, pushed the Italian forces into a hasty retreat, carrying the fight into Albania. Having dealt with the Italians, the Greeks now faced the more daunting prospect of a German attack.

From 6 April 1941, the Germans poured into Greece, and by the twenty-third Greece had surrendered, their prime minister having shot himself while the swastika flew over the Acropolis. British forces in Greece withdrew to Crete, which in turn was also crushed by the Nazis, forcing another evacuation for the British. The Greeks were to suffer terribly under the Germans, enduring routine barbarism and murder (only 2 per cent of Greece's Jewish population survived the war) and large-scale starvation.

Romania's supply of petrol was vital to the German war machine, and in September 1940, Germany disposed of Romania's king, and gave its support to a fascist government, which started on an enthusiastic campaign against the Jews. In November 1940, Romania joined the Axis, and in June 1941 they began their campaign against the Soviet Union.

On 25 March 1941, the Yugoslavian government, under pressure from Hitler, reluctantly signed the Tripartite Pact with Germany, Italy and Japan, but, two days later, following a coup d'état in which the Yugoslavian prince regent was disposed, the new regime refused to ratify it. Furious, Hitler ordered the destruction of Yugoslavia. Attacking on 6 April, Belgrade was flattened with nearly 4,000 civilians killed by 12 April. It took Axis forces only eleven days to force a surrender. The Germans gave Croatia their independence as a fascist republic and the collaborationist Croatian government hounded their Jews with brutal relish. In the remaining part of Yugoslavia, communist partisans, led by Josip Broz ('Tito'), and Chetnik rebels fought the Germans and each other with equal intent.

North Africa: 'A great general'

Mussolini's adventures in North Africa were to prove as fruitless as in the Mediterranean. On 13 September 1940, from their bases in Libya, Italian forces invaded British-controlled Egypt. British and Commonwealth forces, vastly outnumbered, beat the Italians out of Egypt, back into Libya and, along the way, took a number of Libyan coastal towns, including Tobruk, which was to play a strategic and symbolic part in the North African campaign, changing hands several times between the advancing and retreating armies. The British were within striking distance of Libya's capital, Tripoli, but with the Greeks now facing the Germans, Churchill diverted most of the advancing troops from Libya to help in Greece.

Mussolini had become a burden, and in February 1941, Hitler sent to North Africa his ablest soldier, Erwin Rommel, of whom Churchill said: 'We have a very daring and skilful opponent against us, and may I say across the havoc of war, a great general.' Over the next two years the British and Commonwealth armies and the German and Italian forces fought a seesaw war, the Axis pushing the Allies back east into Egypt, then the Allies pushing the Axis back west into Libya. The further one army reached, the further their supply lines were stretched and the easier it became for the other to fight back. One constant thorn in the German side was the Mediterranean island of Malta, from where British forces continuously disrupted the German flow of supplies from Italy to Tripoli. Despite severe bombing, Hitler's attempts to smash the island failed. Britain's King George VI awarded the island, as a collective, the George Cross.

In June 1942, the British had entrenched themselves in the small Egyptian town of El Alamein, sixty miles west of Alexandria. Significantly for the Germans, they were 1,400 miles from Tripoli. The first battle of El Alamein, in July 1942, ended in stalemate. The second battle, with the Allies now led by Field Marshal Bernard Montgomery, or 'Monty', resulted in a Commonwealth triumph. Rommel, his tanks greatly outnumbered and supplies running thin, was, bit by bit, pushed back, the British retaking Tobruk on 13 November.

Five days beforehand, fresh British and American forces had landed to the west in North Africa, in Morocco and Algeria, where they met limited resistance from the Vichy French, who, after only three days, surrendered. Hitler viewed their performance as treacherous and responded by occupying the Vichy-controlled part of France. Montgomery's men eventually captured Tripoli in January 1943, and two months later had chased the Germans further westwards into Tunisia. On 9 March, Rommel was invalided back home, and, soon after, the Allies breached the fortified Tunisian–Libyan border, pushing the Germans into Tunis. Despite Hitler pouring more troops in, and their tenacious defence, the Germans finally surrendered on 13 May 1943. The Allied victory in North Africa prompted Churchill to say: 'This is not the end, nor is it even the beginning of the end, but it is, perhaps, the end of the beginning.'

Germany's Invasion of the Soviet Union: 'The whole rotten structure will come crashing down'

Despite the Nazi–Soviet Pact of August 1939, Hitler's intention was always to invade the Soviet Union. It was, along with the destruction of the Jews, fundamental to his core objectives – *Lebensraum*, or living space, in the east and the subjugation of the Slavic race. This was meant to be a war of annihilation – Russia's non-signing of the Geneva Convention legitimized, in Hitler's view, the enforcement of 'executive measures' in occupied territories. Despite the vastness of Russian territory and manpower, Hitler anticipated a quick victory, hence the lack of provision for winter uniforms. 'You have only to kick in the door,' said Hitler confidently, 'and the whole rotten structure will come crashing down.' Two tons of Iron Crosses were waiting in Germany for those involved with the capture of Moscow.

The Soviets' dismal display against the Finns was proof to Hitler of their military weakness – but Hitler underestimated the Russian ability to learn from their mistakes. He believed that the Russian population would welcome his troops and in many places they did, but instead of harnessing this allegiance, the Germans' brutal methods soon alienated these potential collaborators. He also underestimated the Russians' determination and tenacity; determination that would have existed even without Stalin's infamous 'Not one step back' directive of 28 July 1942, ordering execution for the slightest sign of defeatism. Behind the Soviet front line roamed a second line ready to shoot any retreating cowards or 'traitors of the Motherland'. As Georgi Zhukov, one of Stalin's top generals, said: 'In the Red Army it takes a very brave man to be a coward.'

Stalin's spies had forewarned him time and again of the expected attack, but he refused to believe it. He strenuously forbade anything that might appear provocative to the Germans, even allowing the continuation of Soviet food and metal exports to the Germans, as agreed in the Tripartite Pact, and forbidding the evacuation of people living near the German border and the setting up of defences. So when, at 4 a.m. on 22 June 1941, Operation Barbarossa was launched with over 3 million Axis troops along a 900-mile front, progress was rapid. The date was significant: it was exactly 129 years since Napoleon's ill-fated attack on Russia. Within the first day, one quarter of the Soviet Union's air strength had been destroyed. By the end of October, Moscow was only sixty-five miles away, over 500,000 square miles of Soviet territory had been captured, and as well as huge numbers of Soviet troops and civilians killed, 3 million Red Army soldiers had been taken prisoner of war, and, unlike in the west, the rules of captivity held no meaning for the Germans. A large percentage of Soviet prisoners of war died of malnutrition, disease and brutality.

By the end of June, Finland, Hungary and Albania had all declared war on the Soviet Union. For Finland it was a 'holy war',

an opportunity to avenge their defeat of the previous year. For the first week of the invasion Stalin suffered what is believed to be a mental breakdown, disappearing to his dacha, issuing nothing in the way of direction. When his Politburo came for him, Stalin feared he was about to be arrested. Instead, they came to ask him what to do. Once stirred, Stalin re-emerged. In his first public address since the invasion, on 3 July, Stalin spoke of 'The Great Patriotic War'.

The speed of the German advance soon slowed down – the further they reached, the longer the lines of supply had to become. As Russian forces retreated, they adopted a scorched-earth policy, destroying anything that might be of use to their pursuers – food, crops, livestock and shelter. To add to their increasing discomfort, behind the German advance, groups of Soviet partisans sprang up, hiding away in the unending forests, disrupting the German lines of communication and denting German morale. At the front, for every ten Russian divisions the Germans destroyed, another ten appeared – the reserves of manpower were interminable and soul-destroying for the attackers. When Stalin learnt that Japan, despite signing the Tripartite Pact with Germany and Italy, was not going to renege on the earlier Soviet–Japanese Non-Aggression Pact, he was free to redeploy his troops in the east to face the Germans in the west.

But it was Russia's great ally – 'General Winter' – that changed Russia's fortunes. With autumn came the heavy rains, hampering German progress as vehicles became bogged down in poor roads and mud, and then came the onslaught of winter. Hitler had only provided his troops with summer uniforms, fully expecting victory to come before the onset of the Russian winter. His men suffered terribly in the sub-zero conditions, and with the lack of food and medical supplies, disease spread and morale fell.

As his troops approached Moscow, Hitler diverted the main

thrust south, towards Kiev, citing the capture of crops and oil reserves in the Ukraine (and thereby denying them to the Russians) as more important than the fall of the Soviet capital. Although Germany's lack of natural resources was a constant worry for Hitler, many saw it as a fateful decision, sealing Germany's fate in the Soviet Union. Stalin, meanwhile, was relocating the Soviet Union's factories to the east, and output soared as the war raged on. In December, the German juggernaut ground to a halt, just thirty miles from Moscow with the spires of the Kremlin within view. Hitler's attack on Yugoslavia and Greece had delayed Operation Barbarossa by a month, leaving many of his generals wondering what could have been achieved if they hadn't lost that precious time.

In September, German forces had encircled Leningrad, but Hitler chose to starve it into submission rather than bomb it. Every cat, rat and living animal was eaten, glue was made into soup, and wood for fuel ran out as the city froze. During 872 gruelling days, until 27 January 1944, the city endured an epic siege in which approximately 1,000 civilians died of starvation and the cold each day (in all there were up to a million deaths in Leningrad – more than the total death toll of British soldiers and civilians throughout the war). Limited supplies of food were brought in from the east over Lake Ladoga – by boat during summer and by lorry over the frozen waters during winter – but there was never enough and cannibalism was rife.

War in the Far East: 'Your boys are not going to be sent into any foreign wars'

Pearl Harbor

America had so far maintained an isolationist stance, refusing to be drawn into another European war. While electioneering in October 1940, the American president, Franklin D. Roosevelt, told an audience of parents in Boston: 'Your boys are not going to be sent into any foreign wars.' A month later, he was duly re-elected, the only American president to serve more than two terms. However, despite his isolationist claims, Roosevelt pushed through the Lend-Lease Act in March 1941, supplying the European allies, including the Soviet Union, with huge quantities of material to be paid for in instalments, which by the end of the war amounted to loans worth over $50 billion.

The Chinese contribution to the war is often overlooked; indeed for the Chinese the Second World War began in earnest in 1937.

Japan saw China's growing economy as a threat to their influence. The communists, led by Mao Zedong, and the Chinese nationalists, who had been embroiled in a vicious struggle for dominance, joined forces to fight the Japanese. Japan needed increasing resources to continue the war against China, which, with illusions of imperial greatness, they could not now abandon.

America feared Japan's increasingly aggressive stance in the Far East, and when, in September 1940, Japan signed a Tripartite Pact with Germany and Italy, the USA responded, in July 1941, by freezing Japanese assets and placing an embargo on selling oil to Japan. Japan's economic welfare suffered, but negotiations between the two countries failed.

At six o'clock on a Sunday morning, 7 December 1941, 353 Japanese planes attacked the US fleet docked in the Hawaiian port of Pearl Harbor, 3,400 miles from Tokyo. Four hours later it was over – fourteen ships, including eight battleships, and 400 aircraft destroyed, with 4,700 Americans dead or wounded.

The following day, Roosevelt called 7 December 'a date that will live in infamy'. Congress voted 388 to 1 in favour of war. For Churchill the news gave him the 'greatest joy'. Hitler, too, was delighted, indulging in a glass of champagne. Three days later, on 11 December, during the same week that the first Germans were being taken prisoner of war by the Russians, Hitler (and Mussolini) declared war on the USA.

The Philippines

On the same day as Pearl Harbor, the Japanese also attacked and conquered Thailand and struck at American airbases on the Philippine island of Luzon and British airbases in northern Malaya. Three days later, Japanese planes sank two British warships off the east coast of Malaya – the HMS *Prince of Wales* and *Repulse*. Years later Churchill wrote: 'In all the war, I never received a more direct shock.' On Christmas Day 1941, the British lost Hong Kong to the Japanese. Also in December, American and Filipino forces, led by General Douglas MacArthur, were forced to flee from the capital of the Philippines, Manila. They retreated first to the Bataan Peninsula, then on to the island of Corregidor, when Roosevelt ordered MacArthur out of the Philippines, to Australia. MacArthur complied, though vowing, 'I shall return.'

With no reinforcements available and with the Americans suffering from malaria and low morale, the Japanese took Bataan on 9 April 1942, forcing the 80,000 remaining American and Filipinos on to a seven-day, 65-mile 'Death March' into captivity. One-sixth died en route – shot or bayoneted by their guards. Only a third survived to liberation three years later. Corregidor fell twenty-seven days after Bataan, when the surviving Filipinos were used for live bayonet practice. The Japanese indulged in an orgy of rape, torture and murder against the local population, culminating in the 'razing of Manila'. The Philippines were finally liberated in February 1945.

Burma

On 11 December 1941, the Japanese also landed on the southern tip of the British colony, Burma, determined to block Burmese supplies from reaching China on the Burma Road. They proceeded north, defeating the British and Commonwealth forces in battle and pushing them back. Many Burmese soldiers, discontent with British rule, took the opportunity to desert and join the newly formed national army, fighting alongside the Japanese. On 7 March 1942, the Allies, led by Major-General William Slim, had to abandon the strategically important city of Rangoon, and, having also lost control of the Burma Road, embarked on a 1,000-mile retreat north-west into India, the longest retreat in British military history. But the Japanese in Burma were harassed by guerrilla jungle tactics employed by Burmese still loyal to the British and by British 'Chindits', led by Major-General Orde Wingate, formed specifically for the purpose, with mixed results. The Allies recaptured Rangoon in May 1945, but war in Burma did not end until August, following the Japanese surrender.

Malaya and Singapore

British Malaya was considered a strategic stronghold. During February 1942, Japanese soldiers on bicycles headed south through Malaya, forcing British and Commonwealth troops on to the small island of Singapore on the southern tip of Malaya. The British had concentrated their island defences facing south out to sea, believing the dense jungle to the north to be impenetrable. Unaware of how numerically inferior the enemy was, an impressive bluff perpetrated by the Japanese, the British and Commonwealth troops, led by General Arthur Percival, panicked at the speed of the Japanese advance, and having retreated to Singapore, destroyed the causeway between the mainland and the island. The Japanese merely built a new causeway and poured on to the island. British discipline broke, panic set in, and the cause was lost. On 15 February, the British surrendered, despite Churchill's order that 'No surrender can be contemplated.'

Photographs of Percival walking forlornly towards the Japanese commanders, his colleagues carrying Union Jack and white flags, flanked by Japanese soldiers, summed up the abysmal episode. Over 80,000 British and Commonwealth troops were to spend the rest of the war in captivity. The loss of Singapore was considered the worst humiliation in Britain's military history.

The Battles of Java Sea, Coral Sea and Midway

In the Pacific, the Japanese aimed to conquer the islands north of Australia and sever the supply line between the USA and Australia. In February 1942, the Japanese took control of the oil-rich Dutch East Indies (now Indonesia), defeating an armada of Allied ships at the Battle of Java Sea in the process. Many more Pacific islands fell, and Australia started to look vulnerable, more so when the Japanese sought to take Port Moresby in New Guinea, opposite Australia. However, having broken the Japanese navy codes, the American navy moved to intercept the Japanese fleet, taking them by surprise at the Battle of the Coral Sea, from 4–8 May 1942. It was a battle of aircraft carriers, fought with planes, the first where the opposing fleets never came within sight of each other. The battle ended inconclusively, but the losses sustained by the Japanese hampered a similar battle a month later, during Japan's attempt to take Midway Island. Again, the ability to read their enemy's coded messages played a crucial part in the American victory. The Japanese threat to Australia was removed and the Americans maintained their naval and air superiority throughout the rest of the war, aided by their capacity for war production, which far exceeded that of the Japanese.

Guadalcanal and the Pacific Islands

On one of their many captured islands north of Australia, Guadalcanal, the Japanese began constructing a runway for future sorties south towards Australia. The Americans, having gleaned this information through intelligence, landed a force there on 7 August 1942, the first US ground offensive of the war, capturing the runway without opposition and sending the Japanese scurrying north into the dense jungle on the island. Two days later, the

Japanese navy successfully attacked American ships bringing in supplies, but further attempts failed. Eventually, in February 1943, after the longest battle of the Pacific war, the remaining Japanese evacuated.

The Japanese at War

Had their treatment of local civilians in the countries they conquered been more humane, the Japanese cause may have been furthered, but their conduct and the atrocities inflicted on civilians and prisoners of war were brutal and merciless. Rape, beheading, bayoneting and gruesome torture and medical experiments on human guinea pigs were commonplace. The Japanese considered surrender a shameful act and preferred honour through death than the shame of being taken alive. Therefore, they treated their prisoners barbarically and routinely worked them to death: one quarter, for example, of those detailed to work on the construction of the 250-mile Burma railway died an ignoble death. One in twenty Allied prisoners died at the hands of the Germans, compared to one in four held in Japanese captivity.

The Battles of Stalingrad and Kursk:
The New Field Marshal

Considered important because of its supply of oil, the symbolic significance of Stalingrad (Tsaritsyn was renamed as Stalin's city in 1925) soon outweighed its strategic importance. The Germans started the bombardment of the city on 23 August 1942 and soon after marched in, full of optimism. The Germans, Italians and Romanians fought the Soviets street for street, house for house, sometimes room for room. This, as the Germans called it, was rat warfare, where a strategic stronghold changed sides so many times, people lost count, where the front lines were so close one could throw back a grenade before it exploded, where snipers took their toll on the enemy, and where a soldier's life expectancy was three days – if lucky.

Gradually, from November 1942, the Germans, commanded by General Friedrich Paulus, were encircled by the Soviets who squeezed them tighter and tighter. Supplies, dropped in by the

Luftwaffe, were only a fraction of what was needed. As temperatures dropped to the minus forties, starvation, frostbite, disease and suicide decimated the Germans. Piles of frozen corpses were used as sandbags. Reinforcements, although sent, never came close and Paulus's troops were too weakened to break out from the Soviet encirclement. A few German planes landed within the city and were able to get troops out amidst scenes of panic, with hundreds of men fighting for the few remaining places while being shot at by the Soviets.

In January 1943 Hitler forbade surrender and promoted Paulus to field marshal. No German field marshal had ever surrendered. On 2 February, however, Paulus did. Hitler, 1,000 miles away, was furious. Over a million soldiers on all sides died in the city. Almost 100,000 Axis troops were taken prisoner of war, many later paraded through the streets of Moscow, and only 10 per cent of them returned home after the war. The Germans' defeat at Stalingrad, more than their failure to take Moscow, was the turning point of the whole war.

The city of Kursk, 320 miles south of Moscow, was captured by the Germans in November 1941 and retaken by the Soviets in February 1943. The German field marshal, Erich von Manstein, wanted to recapture it as early as March 1943 as an immediate morale booster after the humiliations at Moscow and Stalingrad, but Hitler wanted to have a new generation of tanks ready before doing so. Intelligence had forewarned the Soviets of Nazi intentions so that by the time Germany did launch a counter-attack, on 4 July, Kursk was fully fortified and prepared. The Germans' hope for a blitzkrieg victory, which depended on the element of surprise, evaporated as the Russians held out and engaged the Germans in a war of attrition, which greatly favoured the Soviets. The climax of the battle took place near a village called Prokhorovka on 12 July, when a thousand tanks and a thousand aircraft on each side clashed on a two-mile front, fighting each other to a standstill. The Battle of Kursk dragged on for another month, but with the German lines continuously disrupted by partisan activity and the Russian capacity to put endless supplies of men and equipment into the fray, the Germans eventually ran out of energy and resources. Hitler, on hearing that the western Allies had landed in Sicily, ordered a withdrawal.

The Holocaust:
'The man with an iron heart'

Hitler's virulent anti-Semitism can be gleaned from reading his autobiographical *Mein Kampf*. The Jew had become the nation's scapegoat for all that was wrong with Germany, including the harsh terms imposed on Germany following her defeat in the First World War. The erosion of Jewish identity began as soon as the Nazis came to power, and by September 1939 half of Germany's Jewish population had migrated. The Nazi disdain for the physically and mentally disabled resulted in a programme of mass euthanasia. Gypsies, homosexuals and all other minorities considered deviant and subhuman by the Nazis fell prey to German brutality. The Nuremberg Laws of 1935 stripped Jews of German citizenship and the violent, state-organized Kristallnacht, the 'Night of Broken Glass', on 9–10 November 1938, razed much of what was left of Jewish identity throughout Germany.

With the outbreak of war, the Nazis immediately began killing or ghettoizing Jews. Over a million Jews had been shot on the edge of grave pits, but the Nazi hierarchy considered the process too time-consuming and detrimental to the mental health of the murder squads, who were often recruited from the local population in conquered areas and willingly collaborated in the killings, but eventually found the task gruelling. Seeking alternative methods, the Germans began experimenting with gas, using carbon monoxide in mobile units, but it was considered too slow and inefficient.

Eventually, after experiments on Soviet prisoners of war in Auschwitz during September 1941, Zyklon B, a gas capable of murdering vast numbers at a time, was introduced throughout all death camps. As well as the extermination camps, there were the labour camps, where inmates were worked to death on, for example, the production of the V-1 and V-2 rockets; and concentration camps, which had been in existence since 1933 for rounding up political opponents of the Nazi regime.

On 20 January 1942, senior Nazis met at Berlin's Lake Wannsee to formalize the 'Final Solution' – the programme to eliminate all Jews – in a two-hour meeting chaired by Reinhard Heydrich, whom Hitler called 'the man with an iron heart'. Heydrich became Hitler's representative in Czechoslovakia and ruled his protectorate with ruthless brutality until his assassination in Prague on 27 May 1942. He died a week later, on 4 June.

In July 1944, Soviet forces liberated the first extermination camps, including Treblinka, and in January 1945, Auschwitz. Only the very weakest prisoners remained; the rest the Germans had taken with them on horrific death marches westwards back to Germany. By the end of the war, 6 million Jews had been murdered, a third of whom were children. Only one-fifth of Jews in German-occupied Europe, including women and children, survived the war.

The Battle of the Atlantic: 'The U-boat peril'

The war at sea began immediately in September 1939 with the Germans sinking merchant ships in the Indian Ocean and the South Atlantic. On 13 December 1939, the Battle of the River Plate in the South Atlantic took place. The German battleship *Graf Spee* damaged a squadron of British ships off the coast of Uruguay, but in doing so was damaged herself. Hitler ordered her captain, Hans Langsdorff, to scuttle her rather than let her fall into enemy hands. Langsdorff followed his orders and the *Graf Spee* was sunk. A week later, Langsdorff, draped in the German flag, shot himself.

In his memoirs, Churchill later confessed: 'The only thing that ever really frightened me during the war was the U-boat peril.' Britain depended heavily on imports – from iron ore and fuel to almost 70 per cent of all her food. Convoys of merchant ships crossing the Atlantic were escorted by the Royal Navy and, as far as it could reach, the RAF. But there was only so far the planes could travel, leaving a 'mid-Atlantic gap', where the convoys were particularly vulnerable to German submarines, or U-boats, which hunted in groups or 'wolf packs'.

On 9 May 1941, a British destroyer attacked a U-boat, and a boarding party managed to capture a German navy (Kriegsmarine) full-scale Enigma coding machine and code books. Although Bletchley Park was already having some success at deciphering the codes, they were now able to do so at will and reroute the convoys in order to avoid the wolf packs. Subsequently, within two months British losses at sea fell by 80 per cent. The discovery helped the Allies throughout the war in all operations.

The champion of U-boats was Commodore Karl Donitz but his superior, Admiral Erich Raeder, advocated the use of large warships. In May 1941, the Kriegsmarine's greatest warship, the *Bismarck*, one-sixth of a mile long, pitted its strength against the equally impressive HMS *Hood*, the pride of the British fleet. On the twenty-fourth, exchanging fire from thirteen miles' distance, the *Hood* was sunk, losing all but three of its 1,400 crew. The *Bismarck* had been damaged, but despite leaking oil, managed to escape the British light cruisers following her. But Bletchley Park intercepted the *Bismarck*'s codes and knew of her destination – Brest, on the western coast of France – where a fleet of British destroyers sought her out and, on 27 May, sank her. Raeder and his warships fell from Hitler's favour and it became the turn of Donitz and his U-boats.

From August 1941, British merchant convoys started delivering supplies to the Soviet Union from bases in Scotland and Iceland. A seventeen-day journey, the Arctic Convoys were fraught with danger, not just from the Kriegsmarine and the Luftwaffe, but the treacherous weather and freezing conditions. However, their contribution to the Soviet war effort, which included tanks and guns as well as raw materials, was invaluable in the fight against Hitler.

During 1943, the British managed to bridge the 'mid-Atlantic gap' with the introduction of 'Very Long-Range Liberators' and with Portugal allowing the use of its airbases in the Azores. Once the USA had entered the war, America was launching more ships than the U-boats could sink and destroying more U-boats than Germany could replace. The RAF was by now successfully destroying U-boats with the aid of radar, and bombing shipyards and docks within Germany. With the Enigma decoding technology still playing its part and with three-quarters of U-boat crewmen being killed in action, the once menacing U-boat had become an 'iron coffin'. Although U-boats continued to be employed throughout the war, the 'Battle of the Atlantic', as Churchill coined it, had been won. From mid-1943, the Kriegsmarine's duties were not so much offensive as defensive, protecting their European coasts from the Allied attack they knew, one day, would come.

The Big Three

The first meeting of the 'Big Three' – Churchill, Roosevelt and Stalin – took place in November 1943 at the Teheran Conference. Stalin, believing that Russia was bearing the brunt of the war, pushed for the western Allies to launch their attack on Germany from the west. The Big Three met again at Yalta, in the Crimea, in February 1945, where arrangements for the post-war world were discussed, and where Stalin promised a declaration of war against Japan three months following the eventual defeat of Germany.

Italy Falls: 'You are the most hated man in Italy'

At the Casablanca Conference of January 1943, Churchill and Roosevelt planned the invasion of Sicily as a prelude to an invasion of Italy, whereby they hoped to remove Mussolini from power, to encourage the Italians to desert Hitler, and equally as important, to force Hitler into diverting troops there from the Soviet Union. The western Allies wanted to avoid a repetition of 1918, when Russia surrendered to Germany, allowing the Germans the luxury of continuing the war on one front. Likening Europe to a crocodile, Churchill referred to Italy as its 'soft underbelly'.

Under the supreme command of Dwight D. Eisenhower, US forces were led by George Patton and British troops by Montgomery, whose conflicting opinions and raging egos threatened to upset Anglo-American relations. Allied troops landed on Sicily on 10 July 1943, where they enjoyed an ecstatic welcome from the islanders. By mid-August, the German forces escaped by crossing over the narrow Strait of Messina on to the Italian mainland.

As a result of the invasion of Sicily, on 24 July, at a meeting of the Fascist Grand Council, Mussolini delivered an impassioned two-hour speech, exhorting his fellow fascists to put up a fight. His plea fell on deaf ears, the Council voting to sign a separate peace with the Allies. The following day, the Italian king, Victor Emmanuel III, dismissed Mussolini, remarking, 'At this moment you are the most hated man in Italy.' Mussolini was immediately arrested by his successor, Pietro Badoglio, and imprisoned. The Italian population rejoiced.

On 8 September, Italy swapped sides and joined the Allies, leaving the Germans to face the Allies without their former partners. Naples fell to Allied forces on 1 October, by which time the Germans had evacuated, destroying much of the city, starving the inhabitants and releasing from prisons criminals who immediately began terrorizing the frightened, malnourished and diseased population. Italy's wish to remain neutral was vetoed by Churchill who demanded Italy's co-operation against the Germans as the price for the 'passage back'.

In mid-September, on Hitler's orders, Mussolini was sprung from his captivity, taken to Germany and returned as the puppet head of a fascist republic in German-occupied northern Italy.

The king promptly deserted his subjects, leaving them leaderless against their former allies. For this act, following the war in 1946, Italy voted to abolish their monarchy for good. On 13 October 1943, Italy reluctantly declared war on Germany. Immediately, the Germans started capturing Italians as prisoners of war, shipping them to internment camps, and began targeting Italian Jews.

The Germans pulled back to the heavily defended Gustav Line, south of Rome, which included the hill-top Benedictine monastery of Monte Cassino. In order for the Allies to progress to Rome, the Gustav Line would have to be breached. In January 1944, in an attempt on Monte Cassino, an amphibious assault landed at Anzio, on the west coast of Italy, thirty miles south of Rome, but German forces rushed in reinforcements and held it in check. On 15 February, 250 Allied bombers flattened the monastery at Monte Cassino, but it still took until 18 May, after weeks of close, hand-to-hand fighting, to breach the Gustav Line, forcing the Germans further north.

The American general, Mark Clark, had orders to give chase and destroy the retreating Germans, but Clark wanted to be the first to capture an Axis capital. Preferring the symbolic glory of taking Rome, Clark ignored his orders and liberated the city on 4 June, after the Germans had already evacuated.

With the end in sight, Mussolini, his mistress, Clara Petacci, and a few followers attempted to escape into Switzerland but they were stopped by Italian partisans. Mussolini's attempts to disguise himself with a Luftwaffe overcoat and helmet had failed, and on 28 April 1945, at Lake Como, Mussolini and Petacci were shot. Their bodies were transported to Milan where they were beaten and urinated upon and finally left to hang upside down for public display.

Despite orders from Hitler to 'stand or die', German resistance finally collapsed and on 2 May 1945, two days after Hitler's death, the Germans in Italy surrendered.

The Bomber Offensive:
'My name is Meyer'

In 1939, Hermann Göring, head of the Luftwaffe, had boasted, 'If bombs drop on Germany, my name is Meyer.' Early RAF bombing missions, however, were considered too dangerous by day and too ineffective by night. On 30 May 1942, Arthur 'Bomber' Harris, appointed commander of Bomber Command in February 1942, organized the destruction of Cologne, using no fewer than a thousand bombers in a determined act of terror against civilians. German war production suffered, but German anti-aircraft guns and the vulnerability of British planes resulted in high casualty rates for the RAF.

In January 1943, Harris joined forces with his American counterpart, Carl 'Tooey' Spaatz, in a renewed initiative in bombing Germany. The RAF bombed cities by night, a policy of 'de-housing', its express purpose to target and demoralize the civilian population (despite evidence during the Blitz that rather than demoralizing, bombing only hardened resolve); while the USAAF bombed industrial and military targets by day. Hamburg was razed in July 1943 by incendiary bombs causing firestorms that engulfed the city, melting cellars, and killing 50,000 people. Numerous other cities were also targeted. But with only one in four aircrew surviving their allocated thirty missions, the attacks were halted. Allied pilots who survived being shot down in Germany were often lynched by the local civilians. The German population called for retaliation, but with Göring's diminishing air power engaged on the Eastern Front, the Luftwaffe lacked the resources to respond.

On 13 February 1945, Bomber Harris sent his planes over Dresden, one hundred miles south of Berlin and brimming with refugees fleeing the Soviets sixty miles away to the east. Dresden, with only minimal anti-aircraft guns, was obliterated. In one night, the city was hit by ten times the number of bombs, and suffered ten times the number of casualties as during the whole of the Blitz, and almost double the number of casualties suffered by Hiroshima after the dropping of the atomic bomb. Churchill questioned Harris's methods of 'bombing German cities simply for the sake of increasing the terror'.

The Normandy Invasion: D-Day

Hitler had long predicted that the Allies would attempt an invasion somewhere in western Europe, and had, accordingly, built a 1,700-mile line of defence from the Netherlands to the Spanish border. Known as the Atlantic Wall, it took two years to construct using slave labour, and once completed, was manned by veterans and cripples of the German army. Hitler pinpointed his prediction to Calais, the shortest distance from England.

Two years before, on 19 August 1942, the Allies had launched an attack on German-occupied France, landing a force at the port of Dieppe. The attack was a disaster and easily fought off by the Germans. However, lessons were learnt – any future attack would have to avoid heavily defended ports. And so, in June 1944, the decision was made to land on beaches.

In planning the invasion of Europe, Montgomery took charge of the British forces, Patton the American forces , with Eisenhower as supreme commander. They decided on a sixty-mile stretch of

Normandy beaches despite the greater distance from England. The lack of harbour facilities was solved by building two gigantic artificial harbours, 'Mulberry Harbours', designed to be towed across the Channel and sunk into place on the beaches. The world's first undersea oil pipeline was constructed, seventy miles long, from the Isle of Wight to Cherbourg. PLUTO (PipeLines Under The Ocean) would eventually pump a million gallons of oil a day into northern France. The French and Belgian Resistance were briefed and instructed. The day before D-Day, the BBC broadcast the poem 'Chanson d'automne' by Paul Verlaine (the nineteenth-century French poet) as the prearranged signal to the Resistance that the invasion would start the following day.

The months preparing for D-Day and the huge armada being gathered in England could hardly escape the attention of German intelligence, so the Allies went to great lengths to mislead the Germans: dummy tanks to fool air reconnaissance, fake radio messages, fake headquarters and even an actor playing Montgomery sent out to North Africa. The deception worked: far fewer Germans were stationed at the beaches because Hitler had them posted across north-west Europe. The British, inspired by Percy Hobart, invented assorted aids to help tanks, dropped into the sea several miles out, to navigate across sea and beaches. Nicknamed 'Hobart's Funnies', the various tanks were designed, between them, to 'swim' on to the shore, clear mines, or roll stretches of canvas out to form a path across the soft sand.

On D-Day, 6 June 1944, Operation Overlord went into action. Gliders and parachutists (and dummy parachutes) landed behind the German lines, capturing the first bit of occupied territory – Pegasus Bridge. Then an armada of 7,000 ships (including 1,200 warships) carrying almost 300,000 men crossed the Channel, the Americans aiming for the beaches named as Utah and Omaha; the British for Gold, Juno and Sword. It was Omaha that saw the greatest struggle; soldiers burdened with heavy kit drowned when deposited from their landing boats in water too deep and others came under immense fire, but eventually, after several hours and through sheer weight of numbers, the beach was secured. The Germans lacked air power, with such commitment on the Eastern Front, and what little they had was soon neutralized by Allied air supremacy.

Hitler, on hearing of the invasion, believed it was a diversionary attack and it was three days before he sent reinforcements. Rommel, in command again of the German forces, had returned to Berlin for the day to celebrate his wife's birthday. On his return, he urged a swift counter-attack, but with insufficient troops and air power, his men fell back as the Allies surged forwards. The Germans were further hampered by partisan activities for which the Germans exacted severe reprisals, obliterating entire villages and murdering their inhabitants. On 27 June, the badly damaged port of Cherbourg was recaptured and the harbour repaired, allowing for easier transportation of men and equipment into France. By the beginning of July, the western Allies had landed over a million men on the Continent.

On 20 July 1944, Hitler survived an assassination attempt in his Wolf's Lair in East Prussia, the 'July Bomb Plot', perpetrated by Nazi officers who hoped to shorten the war with his removal. Hitler, although shaken, suffered only superficial injuries and those responsible were soon rounded up and executed. Rommel, although not directly involved, had previously voiced sympathy for the plan. Once his endorsement came to light, he was given the option of honourable suicide or subjecting himself to humili-ation and the kangaroo court of Nazi justice, and his family deported to a concentration camp. He chose the former, and on 14 October, accompanied by two generals sent by Hitler, poisoned himself. He was, as promised, buried with full military honours, and his family pensioned off.

France Free:
'Liberated by her own people'

On 15 August a secondary Allied attack landed in the south of France and rapidly advanced northwards. It had taken two and a half months, not the planned three weeks, but the road to Paris was finally clear. With the Allies about to enter Paris, Hitler ordered his commander there, Major-General von Choltitz, to destroy much of the city. Choltitz refused and surrendered as, on 25 August, the French general, Philippe Leclerc, led the Allies into the city. They were ecstatically welcomed and the witch-hunt for collaborators began immediately. The following day, De Gaulle made his triumphant return to Paris, marching down the Champs-Élysées, declaring Paris 'liberated by her own people with the help of the armies of France'; a rather fanciful interpretation of the facts. On 3 September, the Allies entered Brussels to an equally joyous reception and by mid-September set foot on German soil for the first time since the war had begun.

But not everything went to plan. In September, Montgomery launched Operation Market Garden, the biggest airborne operation in history, to cut through the Siegfried Line, Germany's line of frontier defences. In doing so, they planned to capture the bridges over the River Rhine, near the town of Arnhem, thereby opening the road to Berlin. Faulty radio transmitters severed communication between the British troops, and determined resistance by the Germans doomed the operation to failure.

On 16 December, with the Germans still retreating, Hitler launched a last-ditch counter-offensive through the Ardennes forest in Belgium in an attempt to cut the advancing Allied fronts into two, and to capture Antwerp, the Allies' key supply point. Despite some initial success in what became known as the Battle of the Bulge, the Germans soon lost the impetus and the Allies, having suffered grievous losses, surged forwards again, pushing the Germans back into the Reich.

While his armies were being pushed further back, and in retaliation for the bombing of German cities, Hitler unleashed on Britain his long-awaited new super weapons – the V-1 (the 'Doodlebug') and V-2. These huge rockets – the V-2 flying faster than the speed of sound – caused much devastation and fear in south-east England. Nothing in Britain's armoury could cope: radar, anti-aircraft guns, fighter planes were all rendered obsolete against these new weapons of terror. But, despite the damage, they arrived too late in the war to make an impact on its outcome.

Stalin was determined his men should take Berlin ahead of the western Allies – it was, after all, his countrymen who had shed the most blood in winning the war. By 25 April, Soviet troops, moving in from the north and south, converged at Potsdam, west of Berlin, thereby encircling the capital, and, on the same day, Soviet and American troops met up on the River Elbe.

The End of the War in Europe:
The Death of a Corporal

The news of Roosevelt's death on 12 April 1945, which came as a personal blow to Churchill, brought temporary joy to Hitler. On 20 April, his fifty-sixth and final birthday, Hitler, the First World War corporal, made his last public appearance in front of a small parade of Hitler Youth boys.

But with the end in sight, Hitler, who had directed fanciful operations of non-existent forces from within his bunker for a number of weeks, married his 33-year-old girlfriend, Eva Braun, and then dictated his last will and testament. The following day, 30 April, the newly-wed couple committed suicide, Eva by cyanide, Hitler with a bullet through his right temple. He died, German radio announced, 'fighting to his last breath against bolshevism'.

On 2 May, Berlin surrendered. On 7 May, Germany surrendered to the western Allies, and, the following day, to the Soviet Union. The war in Europe, at least, had ended.

The End of the War in Japan:
'Complete and utter destruction'

The capitulation of Germany had no effect on Japan's determination to carry on the fight despite their severe losses. One by one, the Japanese lost their Pacific islands as the Americans homed in on the Japanese mainland in a protracted war of attrition. The Japanese fought to the last for each of these islands, preferring death, even by suicide, to surrender. The erosive but ultimately successful fight for the small but strategically important islands of Iwo Jima and Okinawa (both would be used as bases for the air offensive on Japan) is etched on to the American consciousness.

In Burma, Japan's attempt to take the British bases on the Indian border, such as Kohima, failed and General Slim's army of British and Indian troops advanced against the retreating Japanese forces. The Burma Road – supplying the Chinese – was reopened in January 1945 and Rangoon was liberated on 3 May. In the Philippines, the Americans defeated the Japanese navy at the Battle of Leyte Gulf in October 1944, soon followed by the successful recapture of the country, with Manila falling on 23 February 1945. American submarines could now thwart supplies to the Japanese mainland, exacerbating the crisis in Japan.

From the end of 1944, American planes were bombing Tokyo and other cities at will. The American navy had ripped the core out of the Japanese navy, while the Japanese air force, by and large spent, was reduced to the use of aerial suicide attacks, or *kamikaze*, on American ships. Meanwhile, the American naval blockade was having a telling effect on the Japanese supply of food and materials. Defeat was inevitable, but when presented with the opportunity to surrender at the Potsdam Conference in July 1945, and threatened with 'complete and utter destruction', Japan refused.

Faced with a protracted war in the Far East, the Allies took decisive action – on the morning of 6 August, the American plane, *Enola Gay*, dropped an atomic bomb, 'Little Boy', named after Roosevelt, on the city of Hiroshima. The effects were devastating. Two days later, on 8 August, the Soviet Union declared war on Japan, as Stalin had promised at Yalta, but still the Japanese refused to surrender. Three days after Hiroshima, the Americans dropped 'Fat Man', named after Churchill, on Nagasaki. This 'new, most cruel bomb', as Emperor Hirohito called it, finally gave the Japanese the opportunity to surrender without losing honour. The formal surrender took place in Tokyo Bay on board an American battleship on 2 September 1945 – six years and a day after Germany's invasion of Poland.

The Second World War was over.

Appendix One: Key Players

Adolf Hitler 1889–1945

Born in 1889 in Austria, Hitler spent much of his youth in Vienna, living in cheap accommodation, frequenting coffee houses and trying to sell his paintings. Art was his passion and his failure to secure a place at art school plunged him into depression. Resentment of the Jew was rife in the city and Hitler absorbed this anti-Semitism, and like many of his contemporaries, believed, as he wrote in *Mein Kampf*, the Jew to be set apart from 'the rest of humanity'.

At the outbreak of the First World War, Hitler was in Munich. Having managed to avoid conscription into the Austrian army, he signed up to a Bavarian regiment within the German army. He served as a messenger and did so with distinction throughout the war. Having no aspirations for promotion, he finished the war as a corporal, having twice been awarded the Iron Cross and twice wounded – the second time in October 1918 when he was temporarily blinded by mustard gas.

In November 1918, the German government had accepted defeat and it was they, most Germans felt, not the soldier, who had lost the war. The signing seven and a half months later of the Treaty of Versailles confirmed this sense of betrayal, the feeling that the German people had been 'stabbed in the back'.

Among the many small political parties in post-war Germany was the German Workers' Party – or, to use its German abbreviation, DAP – set up in 1919 by a 35-year-old Munich locksmith called Anton Drexler. The DAP, a far-right party that aimed at appealing to the workers, consisted of only about fifty members but their membership cards began at the number 500, to give the impression of more members.

In September 1919, it was to a meeting of this party that Adolf Hitler, at this stage being groomed by the army as a political instructor, was sent to observe and speak. The beer hall meeting consisted of only about twenty attendees, but Hitler's speech so impressed Drexler that he was invited to join the party. With membership number 555 (although he later claimed in *Mein Kampf* that he was the seventh member), he signed his name as 'Hittler'.

Hitler took over the leadership of DAP, changing its name to the National Socialist German Workers' Party, NSDAP, which soon became abbreviated to Nazi. The rise of Hitler had begun.

Winston Churchill 1874–1965

Born in 1874, Churchill took part in the last full-scale cavalry charge during the 1898 Battle of Omdurman in the Sudan. The experience of war embittered him, and he wrote to his mother: 'Our victory was disgraced by the inhuman slaughter of the wounded and Lord Kitchener was responsible for this.'

During the Boer War (1899–1902) he worked as a war correspondent. There he was taken prisoner by the Afrikaaners, but managed to escape.

Originally a Conservative, Churchill swapped sides and from 1910 to 1911 served as Home Secretary for the Liberal Party. During the First World War he was appointed First Lord of the Admiralty and was generally deemed responsible for the British and Commonwealth disaster at Gallipoli. Churchill resigned and served as a battalion commander on the Western Front before being called back by the new prime minister, Lloyd George, to serve in various ministries.

In the 1920s he rejoined the Conservatives and served as Chancellor of the Exchequer from 1924 to 1929.

During the 1930s Churchill remained a Member of Parliament but, mistrusted by all sides as a maverick, was kept out of the Cabinet. Critical of Neville Chamberlain's policy of appeasement, Churchill mocked the Prime Minister's 'peace for our time' declaration, calling the Munich Agreement 'a defeat without war'.

At the start of the Second World War Churchill was recalled to the Admiralty where he took responsibility for the failure of the Norwegian campaign in early 1940. But it was Chamberlain, as prime minister, who fell. Unable to form a coalition government, Chamberlain was forced to resign, to be replaced, ironically, by Churchill.

Following the war Churchill was regaled as Britain's saviour, but nonetheless lost the 1945 election to Labour. He spent his time as leader of the opposition writing his mammoth six-part history of the Second World War, for which, in 1953, he earned the Nobel Prize for Literature.

He served a second term as prime minister from 1951 to 1955, by which time, aged eighty-one, old age and a number of strokes had caught up with him.

He died on 24 January 1965 and was honoured with a state funeral, the details of which Churchill had carefully planned.

Benito Mussolini 1883–1945

As a young man, Mussolini underwent a radical political makeover: an anti-war and anti-nationalistic socialist before the First World

War, by 1921 he had formed a fascist party, the *fasci di combattimento* or 'fighting bands', and was using his blackshirt followers to intimidate opponents into silence.

In 1922 Mussolini threatened to lead a 'March on Rome' unless the Italian king, Victor Emmanuel III, appointed him as prime minister. The king, fearing a civil war, caved in.

As 'Duce' (or Leader), Mussolini wanted to flex his political muscle. He desired an empire. He began in 1935 by invading Ethiopia (then Abyssinia) and, three years later, Albania. The League of Nations protested but did nothing to stop Mussolini scoring easy victories over militarily weak opponents.

During the early 1930s, Mussolini was appalled by Hitler's designs on Austria, but in October 1936 he signed the Berlin–Rome 'Pact of Steel'.

On 10 June 1940, with Germany on the verge of defeating France, Mussolini declared war on the Allies, boasting, 'One moment on a battlefield is worth a thousand years of peace.' But Mussolini's dreams of empire soon unravelled in humiliating fashion, as he failed in his attempt to conquer Greece or British-controlled Egypt, and needed Hitler to bail him out.

By July 1943, the Allies had invaded Sicily and by September of the same year had advanced through mainland Italy. Unable to maintain support, Mussolini was summoned by the king, dismissed, arrested and imprisoned as Italy swapped sides and joined the Allies.

On 12 September 1943, German parachutists executed a daring raid to rescue Mussolini from his Alpine incarceration. On being rescued, Mussolini said of Hitler, 'I knew that my friend would not forsake me!'

Hitler installed Mussolini as the puppet head of a fascist republic in German-occupied northern Italy. Mussolini spent his time ordering the execution of those who had betrayed him at the meeting of the Fascist Grand Council, including his son-in-law and former foreign minister, as well as writing his memoirs.

On 27 April 1945, Mussolini and his mistress, Clara Petacci, together with a few followers, attempted to escape into Switzerland but were apprehended near Lake Como. Mussolini's attempts to disguise himself had failed. The next day, 28 April, Mussolini and Petacci were shot. They died embracing.

The bodies, together with those of their companions, were hung upside down from meat hooks in a Milanese garage and later buried in an unmarked grave.

After the war, Mussolini's body was dug up and, for a whole decade, stored by the Italian government. Finally, in 1956, Mussolini was given a full burial.

Franklin D. Roosevelt 1882–1945

Struck down by polio at the age of twenty-nine, Roosevelt was paralysed from the waist down. He went to great lengths to keep it secret, never appearing in public in his wheelchair, and standing with the support of aides.

He became President in 1932, promising a 'New Deal' to help the USA recover from the turmoil caused by the Great Depression. His reforms did much to stabilize the economy and he was re-elected in 1936 in a landslide victory, winning in all but two states.

With the outbreak of war, Roosevelt promised Britain 'all aid short of war', and in March 1941 introduced the Lend-Lease Act which supplied the European Allies, including the Soviet Union, with huge quantities of material, which by the end of the war amounted to loans worth over $50 billion.

In 1940 Roosevelt was elected to a third term as President, the only President elected more than twice, and was elected for a fourth term in 1944. He died a month before the German surrender, on 12 April 1945.

Joseph Stalin 1879–1953

Born in Georgia on 18 December 1878, Josef Vissarionovich Dzhugashvili is better known to history by his adopted name – Stalin, 'man of steel'. In 1899, at the age of twenty, while training to be a priest, Stalin was expelled from his seminary and from there followed the revolutionary path of a Marxist.

Following the October Revolution in 1917 and the formation of the Soviet Union, Lenin delegated numerous tasks to his eager protégé, culminating in 1922 with Stalin's appointment as General Secretary of the Communist Party. But Lenin began to regret his decision and Stalin's fast-track rise through the party hierarchy, believing Stalin to lack the necessary tact and skill for such a post. In January 1923 Lenin penned a secret memorandum suggesting Stalin's removal from power: 'I am not sure whether [Stalin] will always be capable of using [his] authority with sufficient caution ... Stalin is too rude and this defect ... becomes intolerable in a secretary-general. That is why I suggest that the comrades think about a way of removing Stalin from that post and appointing another man in his stead.'

The other man Lenin had in mind was Stalin's great rival, Lev Trotsky. Together with Trotsky, Lenin was going to use the party congress in April 1923 as his opportunity to have Stalin removed. But in March Lenin suffered a stroke, his third, which confined him to his home and effectively ended his political career.

In January 1924 Lenin died. Trotsky may have been the obvious successor but two of his rivals, Lev Kamenev and Grigori Zinoviev, suppressed Lenin's memorandum and decided to side with Stalin, from whom they felt they had nothing to fear. Trotsky was promptly sidelined and eventually expelled from the party and exiled from the country. But if Kamenev and Zinoviev thought they could tame the Georgian beast they were wrong. Stalin sided with Nikolai Bukharin to have them removed from the party before turning on Bukharin as well. Between 1936 and 1938, Kamenev, Zinoviev and Bukharin were all put through show trials accused of ridiculous charges, sentenced and executed.

Stalin's power was now absolute and he was to rule the Soviet Union unopposed, respected and feared until his death, aged seventy-three, in March 1953.

Bernard Montgomery 1887–1976

The child of a bishop, Montgomery, or 'Monty', fell out with his mother to such an extent he refused to attend her funeral. Training to be an army officer at Sandhurst, he was demoted for having set a fellow student on fire and during the First World War he allegedly captured a German by kneeing him in the testicles.

The early death of his wife from septicaemia, caused by an insect bite, devastated Monty, and from then on he devoted himself entirely to his career.

Self-confident in the extreme, and known for his eccentric headwear, he was adored by his men, especially during the desert campaigns in North Africa during which he made his name. But he frequently clashed with his American counterparts, and perhaps because of his immense pride, took offence easily. His carefully planned assault on Arnhem in 1944 ended disastrously.

When, during his retirement, he was asked to name the three greatest generals in history, he replied, 'The other two were Alexander the Great and Napoleon.'

Erwin Rommel 1891–1944

Respected as a master tactician, Erwin Rommel helped defeat France and the Low Countries and then found lasting fame when sent by Hitler to North Africa where, commanding the Afrika Korps, he earned the sobriquet, the Desert Fox. His Afrika Korps was never charged with any war crimes and prisoners of war were treated humanely. When his only son, Manfred, proposed joining the Waffen SS, Rommel forbade it. In June 1944, Rommel was sent to northern France to help co-ordinate the defence against the Allied Normandy invasion but was wounded a month later when an RAF plane strafed his car. Rommel returned home to Germany to convalesce.

An early supporter of Hitler, Rommel had come round to the view that Hitler's removal was necessary to 'rescue Germany'. He opposed the assassination of Hitler and played no part in the attempt on the Führer's life on 20 July 1944, the 'July Bomb Plot'. However, Rommel's misgivings about Hitler were soon exposed and, once they were, his downfall was inevitable and swift.

On 14 October 1944, Hitler dispatched two generals to Rommel's home to offer the fallen field marshal a bleak choice. Manfred, aged fifteen, was at home with his mother when the call came. He waited nervously as the three men talked in private, and as his father went upstairs to speak to his mother. Finally, Rommel spoke to his son and told him of Hitler's deal.

Writing after the war, Manfred described the scene as his father said, 'I have just had to tell your mother that I shall be dead in a quarter of an hour ... The house is surrounded and Hitler is charging me with high treason. In view of my services in Africa I am to have the chance of dying by poison. The two generals have brought it with them. It's fatal in three seconds. If I accept, none of the usual steps will be taken against my family, that is against you.'

Rommel took the poison and Germany was told that he had

died from 'the injuries sustained during the RAF attack in France'. He was, as promised, buried with full military honours, accorded an official day of mourning, and his family pensioned off.

Writing after the war, Churchill observed that Rommel was deserving of 'our respect, because, although a loyal German soldier, he came to hate Hitler and all his works, and took part in the conspiracy to rescue Germany by displacing the maniac and tyrant. For this, he paid the forfeit of his life.'

Dwight D. Eisenhower 1890–1969

In 1939 Eisenhower, or Ike, was a 49-year-old army major who had never experienced front-line combat. Three years later he was appointed ahead of 360 more senior officers to take command of US forces in Europe. As Supreme Commander of Allied Forces he masterminded the D-Day landings in Normandy and the subsequent battle for France and push into Germany.

He was often resented for his lack of combat experience but was known for his diplomacy and his ability to cope with conflicting egos, bringing about a sense of collaboration between the British and Americans.

In 1953, standing as a Republican, Eisenhower became US President, serving two terms.

Douglas MacArthur 1880–1964

Sixty-year-old MacArthur had taken retirement from his post as Governor of the Philippines when, in 1941, US President Roosevelt recalled him to service to defend the Philippines against the Japanese.

US and Filipino forces were pushed back first to the Bataan Peninsula, then on to the island of Corregidor. Roosevelt ordered MacArthur out of the Philippines, to Australia; he complied, famously vowing, 'I came through and I shall return.'

He did. As Supreme Commander of US Forces in the Pacific, he led the US counter-attack, gradually defeating the Japanese island by island.

During the Korean War he was appointed commander of forces of the United Nations and successfully launched a counter-attack against the North Koreans. However, his bombastic attitude towards the Chinese concerned US President Harry Truman, who, fearing MacArthur's actions might escalate the war further, brought MacArthur home, much to the commander's humiliation.

Hideki Tojo 1884–1948

Tojo advocated closer ties between Japan and Germany and Italy, and in 1940, the three Axis powers signed the Tripartite Pact. A militarist and keen to accelerate the coming of war, Tojo was appointed prime minister in October 1941 and within two months had ordered the attack on Pearl Harbor, thus turning the war into a global conflict. He ruled almost as a dictator, answerable only to Emperor Hirohito.

But as the war turned against Japan, Tojo faced mounting pressure from his government and military hierarchy. Eventually, on 18 July 1944, after a string of losses, the Emperor obliged Tojo to resign.

In September 1945, following Japan's surrender, Tojo tried to resist capture by the Americans by committing suicide by shooting himself in the heart. With US military police pounding at his door, his doctor used a piece of charcoal to draw a circle on Tojo's chest, pinpointing the exact location where Tojo should aim. However, Tojo missed, shooting himself in the stomach. 'I am very sorry it is taking me so long to die', he mumbled as he was arrested. 'I await for the righteous judgement of history. I wished to commit suicide but sometimes that fails.'

Having been nursed back to health, Tojo was tried as a war criminal and found guilty. At his trial, he declared, 'It is natural that I should bear entire responsibility for the war in general, and, needless to say, I am prepared to do so.' He was executed by hanging on 23 December 1948.

Georgi Konstantinovich Zhukov 1896–1974

Instrumental in much of the Red Army's successes during the Second World War, Zhukov held the Germans at bay in Moscow and masterminded the victory at Stalingrad, often considered the turning point of the war.

He led the Red Army to victory at the Battle of Kursk, led the relief of Leningrad and the Red Army's capture of Berlin.

A general of immense quality but with little regard for the human cost of conflict, he finished the war a national hero. But Stalin, jealous of his successes, immediately sidelined him.

Following Stalin's death in 1953, Zhukov returned as Minister of Defence, having helped Khrushchev secure his position as leader. But in 1957, he fell foul of Khrushchev and was relieved of all responsibilities.

Appendix Two:
Timeline of World War Two

1939

1 September	Germany invades Poland.
3 September	Britain and France declare war on Germany.
17 September	Soviet Union invades eastern Poland.
27 September	Surrender of Warsaw.
30 November	Soviet Union invades Finland.
13 December	Battle of River Plate in the South Atlantic.

1940

12 March	Finland signs peace treaty with Soviet Union.
9 April	Germany invades Denmark and Norway.
10 May	Germany invades Belgium, Holland and Luxembourg.
10 May	Winston Churchill becomes British prime minister.
13 May	Bombing of Rotterdam.
15 May	Holland surrenders to Germany.
26 May	Start of the Dunkirk evacuation.
28 May	Belgium surrenders to Germany.

10 June	Capitulation of Norway.
10 June	Italy declares war on Britain and France.
14 June	Germans occupy Paris.
18 June	Soviets annex Baltic states.
22 June	France signs armistice with Germany.
30 June	Germany begins occupation of the Channel Islands.
3 July	British sink French fleet docked in Mers-el-Kebir, Algeria.
11 July	Pétain becomes head of French Vichy government.
13 August	Battle of Britain begins.
13 September	Italy invades Egypt.
15 September	Climax of Battle of Britain.
27 September	Germany, Italy and Japan sign Tripartite Pact.
7 October	German army moves into Romania.
28 October	Italy invades Greece.
14 November	Bombing of Coventry.
14 November	Greek army repels Italians back into Albania.
22 November	Italian army defeated by Greeks.
9 December	British offensive begins in North Africa.

1941

22 January	British take Tobruk.
11 March	USA passes Lend-Lease Bill.
25 March	Yugoslavia signs Tripartite Pact.
27 March	Yugoslavian government overthrown – Yugoslavia leaves Pact.

30 March	German Afrika Korps begins offensive in North Africa.
6 April	Germany invades Yugoslavia and Greece.
12 April	Germans occupy Belgrade.
13 April	Soviet Union and Japan sign neutrality pact.
17 April	Yugoslav army surrenders to Germans.
27 April	Germans capture Athens.
20 May	German airborne invasion of Crete.
24 May	The HMS *Hood* is sunk.
27 May	The *Bismarck* is sunk.
31 May	British forces in Crete defeated.
22 June	Operation Barbarossa – Germany invades Soviet Union.
22 June	Italy and Romania declare war on Soviet Union.
26 June	Finland declares war on Soviet Union.
7 July	German forces enter Estonia.
16 July	Germans capture Smolensk.
21 August	First Arctic Convoy to Russia leaves Iceland.
28 August	German forces take Tallinn.
8 September	Siege of Leningrad starts.
19 September	Germans capture Kiev.
24 October	Germans capture Kharkov.
3 November	Germans capture Kursk.
5 December	Germans abandon attack on Moscow.
7 December	Japanese attack on Pearl Harbor.
7 December	Japan invades Malaya.
8 December	USA and Allies declare war on Japan. (Soviet Union remains neutral.)

10 December	British battleships *Prince of Wales* and *Repulse* sunk off Malaya.
11 December	Germany (and Italy) declares war on USA.
11 December	Japan attacks Burma.
25 December	Japanese capture Hong Kong.

1942

2 January	Japanese capture Manila.
13 January	Soviets recapture Kiev.
21 January	Japan invades Burma.
15 February	Singapore falls to the Japanese.
27 February	Battle of Java Sea.
8 March	Japanese occupy Rangoon.
9 March	Japanese conquest of Java completed.
9 April	Japanese take Bataan.
30 April	Japanese close Burma Road.
6 May	Fall of Corregidor and surrender of US forces in the Philippines.
4–8 May	Battle of the Coral Sea.
27 May	Japanese complete conquest of Burma.
28 May	Germans defeat Soviets at Kharkov.
30 May	RAF bombs Cologne.
4 June	Battle of Midway.
1 July	First Battle of El Alamein begins.
7 August	US forces land on Guadalcanal.
19 August	Britain's Dieppe Raid.
23 August	Stalingrad offensive begins.
23 October	Second Battle of El Alamein begins.
8 November	Allies invade French North Africa.
11 November	Germans occupy Vichy France.

1943

14 January	Casablanca Conference opens.
23 January	British enter Tripoli.
2 February	German surrender at Stalingrad.
8 February	Soviets recapture Kursk.
19 April	Jewish uprising in Warsaw Ghetto begins.
7 May	Allies take Tunis.
13 May	Axis forces in North Africa surrender.
16 May	Jewish uprising in Warsaw Ghetto suppressed.
4 July	Battle of Kursk begins.
10 July	Allies land in Sicily.
25 July	Overthrow and imprisonment of Mussolini.
17 August	Allied conquest of Sicily complete.
23 August	Soviets recapture Kharkov.
3 September	Italy signs armistice.
3 September	Allies land in southern Italy.
8 September	Italy surrenders. Germans occupy Rome.
12 September	Mussolini rescued.
23 September	Mussolini declares fascist government in northern Italy.
25 September	Soviets retake Smolensk.
1 October	Allies capture Naples.
13 October	Italy declares war on Germany.
6 November	Soviets retake Kiev.
28 November	Teheran Conference opens.

1944

22 January	Allies land at Anzio.

27 January	End of Leningrad siege.
15 February	Allies destroy monastery of Monte Cassino.
18 March	RAF bombs Hamburg.
7 April	Japanese attack Kohima.
18 May	Allies take Monte Cassino.
4 June	Allies enter Rome.
6 June	Operation Overlord – Allied invasion of Normandy.
13 June	German V-1 offensive begins against Britain.
27 June	US forces capture Cherbourg.
20 July	Attempted German assassination of Hitler.
1 August	Polish uprising in Warsaw.
15 August	Allies invade southern France.
25 August	Allies liberate Paris.
3 September	Allies liberate Brussels.
4 September	Allies liberate Antwerp.
5 September	Soviet Union declares war on Bulgaria.
8 September	Bulgaria surrenders to Soviet Union.
8 September	German V-2 offensive begins against Britain.
17 September	Operation Market Garden – Allied airborne assault on Holland.
21 September–2 October	Battle of Leyte Gulf.
26 September	Estonia occupied by Soviet Union.
1 October	Soviets enter Yugoslavia.
2 October	End of Warsaw uprising.
4 October	Allies land in Greece.
14 October	Allies liberate Athens.

19 October	US forces invade Philippines.
20 October	Liberation of Belgrade.
23 October	Soviets enter East Prussia.
4 November	Surrender of Axis forces in Greece.
16 December	German attack through Ardennes – Battle of the Bulge begins.

1945

1 January	Germans withdraw from Ardennes.
17 January	Soviets liberate Warsaw.
25 January	Battle of the Bulge ends in German defeat.
26 January	Soviets liberate Auschwitz.
27 January	Burma Road reopened.
4 February	Allies take Manila.
4 February	Yalta Conference opens.
13 February	RAF bombs Dresden.
19 February	Japanese evacuate Mandalay.
19 February	US troops invade Iwo Jima.
23 February	US forces retake Manila.
7 March	US forces cross the Rhine.
17 March	US troops capture Iwo Jima.
21 March	British retake Mandalay.
1 April	US troops invade Okinawa.
11 April	Soviets and Yugoslavs sign treaty.
12 April	US President Roosevelt dies, replaced by Harry Truman.
23 April	Soviets enter Berlin.
25 April	Soviet and US forces meet at the River Elbe.
28 April	Mussolini captured by partisans and executed.

30 April	Hitler commits suicide.
2 May	German forces in Italy surrender.
3 May	British retake Rangoon.
4 May	German forces in Holland, Denmark and north-west Germany surrender.
7 May	German unconditional surrender to the west.
8 May	German unconditional surrender to the east.
9 May	Liberation of Channel Islands.
22 June	US forces capture Okinawa.
16 July	Potsdam Conference opens.
6 August	Atomic bomb dropped on Hiroshima.
8 August	Soviet Union declares war on Japan.
9 August	Atomic bomb dropped on Nagasaki.
14 August	Japan agrees to surrender.
2 September	Formal Japanese surrender.

Got Another Hour?

History in an Hour is a series of eBooks to help the reader learn the basic facts of a given subject area. Everything you need to know is presented in a straightforward narrative and in chronological order. No embedded links to divert your attention, nor a daunting book of 600 pages with a 35-page introduction. Just straight in, to the point, sixty minutes, done. Then, having absorbed the basics, you may feel inspired to explore further. Give yourself sixty minutes and see what you can learn…

To find out more visit http://historyinanhour.com or follow us on twitter: http://twitter.com/historyinanhour

1066: History in an Hour by Kaye Jones

Covering the major events of the year 1066, this is a clear account of England's political turmoil during which the country had three different kings and fought three large-scale battles in defence of the kingdom, including the infamous Battle of Hastings.

The Afghan Wars: History in an Hour by Rupert Colley

A comprehensive overview of the wars that have been fought in Afghanistan for almost four decades, including the politics of the Taliban, why Osama Bin Laden was so significant, and why it is still so hard to achieve peace in the country.

The American Civil War: History in an Hour by Kat Smutz

A clear account of the politics and major turning points of the war that split the country in half as the northern and southern states fought over the right to keep slaves, changing American culture forever.

American Slavery: History in an Hour by Kat Smutz

A broad overview of the major events in the history of American slavery, detailing the arrival of the first slaves, the Southern plantations, the Civil War, and the historical and cultural legacy of slavery in the United States.

Ancient Egypt: History in an Hour by Anthony Holmes

A succinct exploration of the historic rise of Egyptian civilisation and its influence on the world, covering Egyptian gods, mummification and burial rituals, and the Pyramids of Giza.

Black History: History in an Hour by Rupert Colley

A clear overview of the long and varied history of African Americans, including everything from slavery, the Civil War and emancipation to the civil rights movement and the Black Panther Party.

The Cold War: History in an Hour by Rupert Colley

A succinct overview of the politics of the non-violent war, from the end of World War II to the collapse of the USSR in 1991, as Russia and America eyed each other with suspicion and hostility.

Dickens: History in an Hour by Kaye Jones

A comprehensive overview of the life of arguably Britain's most successful and beloved writer, including the poverty of his childhood, the evolution of his novels, his tours of Europe and America, and his occasionally scandalous private life.

George Washington: History in an Hour by David B. McCoy

The essential chronicle of George Washington's life, from his middle-class Virginian upbringing to his unanimous election as America's first president, and the prominent role he played in shaping America as we know it today.

The Gunpowder Plot: History in an Hour by Sinead Fitzgibbon

An engaging account of the infamous plot by a group of Catholic traitors, led by Guy Fawkes, to blow up the Houses of Parliament and James I, including details of the motives behind their drastic actions and how the plot came to be discovered.

Henry VIII's Wives: History in an Hour by Julie Wheeler

An inclusive introduction to the six diverse personalities of Henry VIII's wives, the events that led them to their individual fates, and the different impacts they each had on King and country.

Hitler: History in an Hour by Rupert Colley

A coherent overview of Hitler's early life, service in World War I, rise to the top of the Nazi Party and eventually the head of state, covering all the key moments of the dictator's life through to his death and the crumbling of his empire.

JFK: History in an Hour by Sinead Fitzgibbon

A comprehensive insight into the life of America's youngest elected president, assassinated barely one thousand days into his presidency, examining his navigation of the Space Race, his sympathies with the civil rights movement, and the chronic illness that affected him throughout his life.

The Medieval Anarchy: History in an Hour by Kaye Jones

A look at the unprecedented chaos and disorder that followed the death of King Henry I, leading to England's first, and often forgotten, civil war, as well as an overview of the plots and violence that ensued during this nineteen-year bloody conflict.

Nazi Germany: History in an Hour by Rupert Colley

A concise explanation which covers the major events behind the Nazi Party's climb to power, what it was like to live in Nazi Germany, and how Hitler brought the world into war.

The Queen: History in an Hour by Sinead Fitzgibbon

A compelling history of the UK's second-longest-reigning monarch, covering her 1953 coronation to her Diamond Jubilee in 2012 and examining her long reign, during which the British Empire has transformed.

The Reformation: History in an Hour by Edward A. Gosselin.

A concise look at the spread of religious dissidence across Europe in the sixteenth century, including the events that caused people to question the ideas of the established Catholic Church and the resulting wars, migration and disunity.

The Russian Revolution: History in an Hour by Rupert Colley.

Covering all the major events in a straightforward overview of the greatest political experiment ever conducted, and how it continues to influence both Eastern and Western politics today.

The Siege of Leningrad: History in an Hour by Rupert Colley.

A broad account of one of the longest sieges in history in which over the course of 900 days the city of Leningrad resisted German invasion, contributing to the defeat of the Nazis at the cost of over one million civilian lives.

South Africa: History in an Hour by Anthony Holmes

A fascinating overview of South Africa's history of oppression and racial inequality and how after years of violence and apartheid, Nelson Mandela, the country's first black President, led the country to unite and become the 'Rainbow Nation'.

Stalin: History in an Hour by Rupert Colley

A succinct exploration of Joseph Stalin's long leadership of the Soviet Union, covering his rise to power, his role in the Russian Revolution, and his terrifying regime that directly and negatively affected the lives of so many.

Titanic: History in an Hour by Sinead Fitzgibbon

An account of the catastrophe, including the failures of the White Star Line, the significance of class and the legacy of the disaster in Britain and America.

The Vietnam War: History in an Hour by Neil Smith

A clear account of the key events of the most important Cold War-era conflict, including the circumstances leading up to the Vietnam War, the deadly guerrilla warfare, the fall of Saigon and the backlash of anti-war protests in America.

World War One: History in an Hour by Rupert Colley

A clear overview of the road to war, the major turning points and battles, and the key leaders involved, as well as the lasting impact the Great War had on almost every country in the world.

Printed by RR Donnelley at Glasgow, UK